Chasmosaurus

Written by Rupert Oliver
Illustrated by Bernard Long

Library of Congress Cataloging in Publication Data

Oliver, Rupert.
  Chasmosaurus.

  Summary: Describes a day in the life of the horned Chasmosaurus and discusses its physical characteristics, habits, and natural environment.
    1. Chasmosaurus—Juvenile literature.
  [1. Chasmosaurus.   2. Dinosaurs]   I. Long, Bernard, ill.
  II. Title.
  QE862.O65O445   1986   567.9′7   85-30050
  ISBN 0-86592-218-7

Rourke Enterprises, Inc.
Vero Beach, FL 32964

Dimorphodon

Brachiosaurus

Dilophosaurus

Lystrosaurus

Rutiodon

Chasmosaurus

Mamenchisaurus

Plateosaurus

Chasmosaurus

Protoceratops

The twittering of a single bird broke the silence of
the early morning. More and more voices joined
in until the cool air was filled with a resounding
chorus. As the dawn broke in the east the singing
subsided and only the occasional notes drifted
through the trees.

Underneath a particularly large tree a slow movement disrupted what was otherwise a still scene. A huge, four-legged dinosaur rose to his feet and shook his head. Chasmosaurus sniffed the air. It smelled clean and fresh. It would be another long, hot day. Chasmosaurus grunted his satisfaction as the warming rays of the sun broke through and bathed him in light. Other members of his herd began to stir for the coming day.

The herd moved out from its resting place beneath the tree. Chasmosaurus was thirsty and the herd drifted toward a stream. A sudden itching by his hind leg worried Chasmosaurus, but he could not reach it to scratch. As he drank, the itching became worse and worse. An insect had planted its egg in Chasmosaurus' hide some days earlier. Now the egg had hatched and the larva was burrowing through Chasmosaurus' skin to reach a vein so that it could suck blood.

Chasmosaurus began to rub his leg against a tree in the hope of relieving the itching. It only got worse. Chasmosaurus kept scratching until the flesh was raw and the larva killed by the pressure. His skin stung, but at least the itching was gone.

As Chasmosaurus was savoring the relief from the infuriating insect a movement caught his eye. Slinking along the far side of the stream was a group of two legged dinosaurs. Chasmosaurus looked at them more carefully. Then he recognized them as Dromaeosaurs. Chasmosaurus was filled with fear and terror. He had seen the way Dromaeosaurs hunted before and it spelled danger for him and his herd.

Chasmosaurus bellowed out a roar signalling
his terror to the herd. Instinctively, the herd drew
closer together and Chasmosaurus hurried to join
them.

The two young Chasmosaurs cowered to the
rear while Chasmosaurus and his fellow adults
bunched together in a ring. They faced outward and
lowered their heads. The Dromaeosaurs advanced
toward the Chasmosaurs. The pack of hunters
moved cautiously in front of the herd. The solid line
of horns and frills which faced the Dromaeosaurs was
too much.

After some growling and loud roaring the
Dromaeosaurs lost interest in the Chasmosaurs.
They only stood a chance against armored dinosaurs
if they could catch one on its own. Then, one of the
Dromaeosaurs gave a peculiar growl and all the
pack turned to look toward the stream.

Coming across the stream was a large Parasaurolophus and it had not seen the hungry Dromaeosaurs. Instinctively, the Dromaeosaurs crouched down so that they would not be seen. The Parasaurolophus came closer and closer until suddenly it saw the Dromaeosaurs. It was too late. The Dromaeosaurs could run much faster than the Parasaurolophus. The fierce little hunters soon caught up with their much larger prey. The attacking Dromaeosaurs leaped agilely at the Parasaurolophus, slashing ferociously with their long, sharp claws. It was not long before they had killed the Parasaurolophus and were eating its flesh.

The Chasmosaurs edged slowly away from the dangerous meat eaters. As they moved off, a large Albertosaurus lumbered past them. Albertosaurus had smelled the blood of the Parasaurolophus. Perhaps he could frighten the Dromaeosaurs away and eat his fill of their food.

As soon as the herd was out of sight of the
Dromaeosaurs, it spread out again. Chasmosaurus
moved toward a tasty looking group of bushes. A
sudden thud startled him. Perhaps there was more
danger here. Chasmosaurus began to edge quietly
backward with his head lowered. Then, he heard the
familiar enraged call of a Ceratopsian.

Chasmosaurus pushed around the bushes and found the source of the noise. Two male Styracosaurs were fighting each other. With heads lowered, they were charging at each other and butting with their horns.

A little way off, Chasmosaurus could see a large clump of juicy palms, his favorite food. Chasmosaurus called out in pleasure to the rest of his herd. They followed him over toward the succulent palms.

Already amongst the palms was an Alamosaurus. The long necked Sauropod was feeding on the leaves at the tops of the highest palms. This meant it would not disturb the Chasmosaurs. They ate the leaves and shoots much lower down the plants. As Chasmosaurus sliced off leaf after leaf, he greedily lapped up the delicious juice which flowed from the damaged plant. This was the reason why Chasmosaurus liked palms so much. No other plant gave juice in this way.

Chasmosaurus steadily munched away at the palms. All the time he was moving deeper into the clump of vegetation. After taking hold of a particularly juicy leaf, Chasmosaurus stopped in surprise. Behind the palm had been a Troödon.

The Troödon had just caught a small
mammal which it was holding in its jaws. The
Troödon was even more surprised than the
Chasmosaurus to be disturbed during its meal.
Keeping a firm hold on its prey the Troödon
scampered off through the foliage. Chasmosaurus
carried on eating for a while. Then, he realized that
he was some way from the herd. He felt lonely and
unprotected so he moved back toward the other
Chasmosaurs.

The sun was starting to go down in the West when Chasmosaurus emerged from the palms with the rest of his herd. A Euoplocephalus brushed past Chasmosaurus as it sought a place to bed down for the night. The herd of Chasmosaurs lay down on the edge of the palm clump as the sky turned a deep shade of red. Chasmosaurus was tired and he would need a good night's rest before the next day.

The soft grunts of the sleeping Chasmosaurs whispered through the air as the small mammals crept out to hunt insects and the birds winged home to their nests.

Chasmosaurus and Late Cretaceous Montana

Skeleton of Chasmosaurus

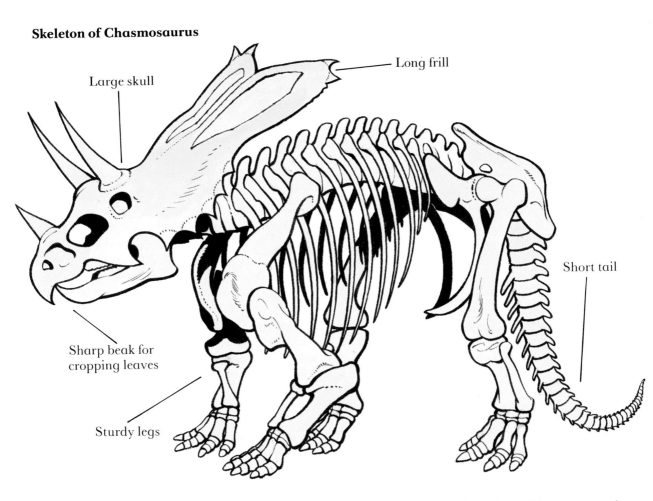

Large skull

Long frill

Sharp beak for cropping leaves

Sturdy legs

Short tail

The time of Chasmosaurus

Scientists have divided the entire history of the world into eras and each era into a number of periods. Between 225 million years ago and 65 million years ago was the Mesozoic Era, the Age of the Dinosaurs. This immense stretch of time has been divided into three periods; the Triassic, the Jurassic and the Cretaceous. The fossils of Chasmosaurus have been found in the most recent rocks of the most recent of these periods, the Cretaceous. This means that it lived about 70 million years ago.

The land of Chasmosaurus

Chasmosaurus fossils have been found in a number of places on the North American continent. They have turned up as far apart as New Mexico and Alberta. The story in the book takes place in what is now Montana about 70 million years ago. All the animals in the story lived in roughly the same place and at the same time as

Chasmosaurus. At that time, Montana, and North America as a whole, was quite different from how it appears today. The Rocky Mountains were only just beginning to be created. They were still fairly low and had not reached the spectacular, snow covered heights which we see today. There is also some evidence to suggest that a shallow, inland sea stretched from the Gulf of Mexico to Hudson Bay, flooding much of what are today the Great Plains, while a broad reach of ocean separated North and South America. Conversely, it is thought that western North America may have been joined to eastern Asia in some way.

Family tree of Chasmosaurus

Chasmosaurus belonged to one of the most distinctive of all dinosaur families. It was a Ceratopsian. The Ceratopsians evolved very late in the Age of the Dinosaurs. The first Ceratopsian was Protoceratops which lived in eastern Asia about 90 million years ago. It was much smaller than Chasmosaurus and had no horns at all. Over the millions of years the line of the Ceratopsians became one of the most numerous and diversified in dinosaur history. There quickly evolved two main lines of evolution; the long frilled Ceratopsians and the short frilled Ceratopsians. Chasmosaurus belonged to the long frilled group, but Styracosaurus, which appears in our story, was a short frilled Ceratopsian. The Ceratopsians continued to evolve and to thrive, producing dozens of species, right up until the end of the Mesozoic Era when they all became extinct. Exactly why such a successful group should die out so completely nobody is really certain.

Other plant eaters

The late Cretaceous rocks in which the fossils of Chasmosaurus have been found have also yielded many other fossils. Some of the animals whose fossils turn up in rocks of the same age and location have been included in the story, but many others have been found. Alamosaurus, as its name might suggest, was first found in Texas and was named after the famous Alamo. It was a Sauropod and is therefore unusual in that it survived into the late Cretaceous. Most Sauropods, such as Diplodocus and Brontosaurus, had died out millions of years earlier. Parasaurolophus, like Chasmosaurus, belonged to a group which evolved quite late in the Age of the Dinosaurs. It was a

Hadrosaur. This group of two legged plant eaters appeared at about the same time as the Ceratopsians and likewise evolved into many species. Most members of the group are distinguished by the curious growths on their heads. Nobody is really sure what these were used for. Euoplocephalus was one of the commonest dinosaurs from Late Cretaceous Montana and was a close relative of the more famous Ankylosaurus. It had a strong, protective covering of bony armor along the top of its head, body and tail.

Meat eaters

Many types of carnivorous dinosaurs lived at the same time as Chasmosaurus. Perhaps the most dangerous was Dromaeosaurus. This rather small dinosaur was a very fast runner and agile hunter. Its main weapon was the large, sickle-shaped claw on its hind feet. These were formidable weapons and enabled Dromaeosaurus to bring down large animals, such as Parasaurolophus. The much larger Albertosaurus was a close relative of the famous Tyrannosaurus Rex. Scientists disagree about the role of such large meat eaters. Some think of them as formidable hunters. Other scientists say that Albertosaurus and its like were too clumsy to hunt as did the Dromaeosaurs and think that such dinosaurs were mere scavengers.

Other Ceratopsians

Triceratops, which lived after Chasmosaurus

Protoceratops, which lived before Chasmosaurus